I0532112

# Emotional Intelligence

*A Step by Step Guide to Improving Your EQ, Controlling Your Emotions and Understanding Your Relationships*

**Jessica Greiner**

including specific information will be considered an illegal act irrespective of if it is done electronically or in print. This extends creating a secondary or tertiary copy of the work or a recorded copy and is only allowed with an express written consent from the Publisher. All additional right reserved.

The information in the following pages is broadly considered to be a truthful and accurate account of facts, and as such any inattention, use or misuse of the information in question by the reader will render any resulting actions solely under their purview. There are no scenarios in which the publisher or the original author of this work can be in any fashion deemed liable for any hardship or damages that may befall them after undertaking information described herein.

Additionally, the information in the following pages is intended only for informational purposes and should thus be thought of as

# Table of Contents

# Introduction

Are you looking for a way to stand out from the crowd at work while also improving your relationships with your friends and loved ones?

Would you be interested in learning a skill that practically screams management potential, but will also help you be more universally loved by your coworkers?

Would you be interested in a skill that helps you know what other people are thinking and feeling, even if they aren't really sure of it themselves?

If you answered yes to either of these questions, then *Emotional Intelligence: A Step by Step Guide to Improving Your EQ, Controlling Your Emotions and Understanding Your*

Emotional Intelligence

*Relationships* is the book you have been waiting for.

While you may not yet be familiar with the concept of emotional intelligence, rest assured that it is affecting your everyday life in ways that you cannot yet fathom. What's more, while you may not have heard about it, rest assured that employers have which means that if it's not an area you have recently brushed up on, then you could very well be missing out on future job opportunities as a result.

In addition to ensuring you are streets ahead when it comes to the job market, improving your emotional intelligence will also improve virtually every aspect of your relationships with the people around you. While before you may have had a hard time empathizing with those around you, with proper emotional intelligence training you will find that not only do you understand the point of view of other's more easily, you will be able to quickly put together solutions that take everyone's feelings into account as well.

The following chapters will fill you in on just what all the fuss is about regarding emotional intelligence while also discussing everything you need to know to not only understand the basics of emotional intelligence but become an expert at putting it to good use as well. First, you will learn all about what emotional intelligence is, how it compares to intellectual intelligence along with the elements that are crucial to its success. Once you have an understanding of what you are working for, the next thing you will learn is how to test your own level of emotional intelligence, so you know what you are working with to start.

From there, you will find a step-by-step guide to improving your emotional intelligence, starting with a number of exercises that you can do to prime the pump and get your emotional juices flowing. Next, you will learn all about improving your self-awareness, self-expression, following your passion, self-management and relationship management before topping things off with a discussion of how to best apply emotional intelligence in the workplace. Finally, you will find a list of mistakes that many people make when trying to improve their emotional intelligence, along with easy ways to avoid these common pitfalls.

There are plenty of books on this subject on the market, thanks again for choosing this one! Every effort was made to ensure it is full of as much useful information as possible, please enjoy!

# Chapter 1:
# Emotional Intelligence Basics

If you find it harder and harder each year to make new, meaningful connections with the people you meet each day, the good news is you are not alone. The ever-increasing emphasis on screens makes finding this type of connection more difficult than ever before. If you feel as though your inability to connect with others goes deeper than that, however, then you may need to improve your emotional intelligence. While not discussed nearly as often as traditional intelligence, emotional intelligence is just as important to your everyday life as it will allow you to more easily turn thoughts into actions, make an instant connection with other people and generally ensure you make better decisions throughout your life.

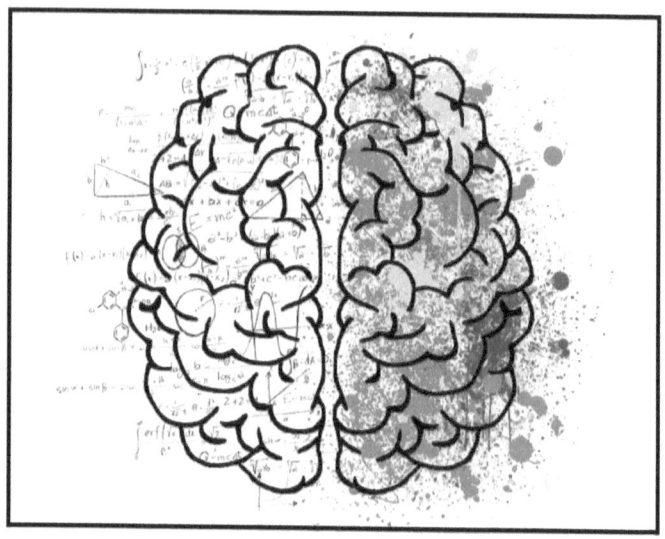

More specifically, emotional intelligence can be seen as the ease with which a person is able to access emotion to understand, identify and manage a wide variety of situations including those that require you to make an empathetic connection with others, communicate succulently or simply to reduce your overall level of stress. Emotional intelligence also makes it easier to understand nonverbal cues including body language which is extremely beneficial in both social and business circles.

## Chapter 1: Emotional Intelligence Basics

Generally speaking, emotional intelligence can be broken down into three distinct skills. First, is the emotional awareness, or the ability to understand the emotions that other people are experiencing. Second, is the ability to harness your emotions, or the emotions of others, for specifics tasks. Third, is the ability to manage your emotions as needed. While it may all seem very self-explanatory when it is written out in this way, the truth of the matter is that those with high emotional intelligence are exceedingly rare.

**A brief history**

While it was first discussed in the 1960s, the concept of emotional intelligence didn't gain popularity until the 90s, thanks to the work of two men, John Mayer and Peter Salovery. In their revolutionary whitepaper titled *Emotional Intelligence,* they introduce the idea that emotional intelligence, which they dubbed EQ, was just as important as IQ, if not even more so. What's more, they also proved that EQ can be measured, just as IQ can. According to their analysis, EQ is broken down into four different aspects, managing emotions, understanding emotions, using emotions and perceiving emotions.

Salovey and Mayer even went so far as to say that EQ is more than just a cognitive ability and that it could be applied to IQ as well. Their research was followed up by that done by Daniel Goleman, who released the book *Emotional Intelligence: Why It Can Matter More than IQ* in 1995. This book would remain on the *New York Times* Best Seller List for more than 18 months and would ultimately go on to be published in more than 40 languages. It essentially covered the same concepts like the theory that Salovey and Mayer put forth, just expressed in a way that people could use in their everyday lives.

## Chapter 1: Emotional Intelligence Basics

### Key elements of emotional intelligence

While there are plenty of different theories out there when it comes to emotional intelligence, there are some core elements that everyone seems to agree on including social skills, empathy, motivation, self-regulation, and self-awareness, each of which is discussed in detail below.

*Self-awareness*: Simply put, self-awareness is the ability to recognize your own intuition, resources, preferences, internal states, and overall emotions. It can be thought of as the place where increasing your EQ will really start as increasing your self-awareness naturally starts you down the path towards improving your emotional intelligence as well. This is because understanding your own emotions is crucial to managing them successfully. Self-awareness will also make it easier to empathize with others.

Emotional Intelligence

***Self-regulation****:*    Self-regulation    springs directly from self-awareness as you must first be in sync with your emotions, while also understanding their causes before you can hope to regulate them effectively. Thinking before you act is the key to controlling your emotions and will also make it easier to withhold judgment of others at the moment as well. Generally speaking, intense situations tend to cause most people to react in an emotional way, such as taking a series of unfortunate events personally or responding to constructive criticism with unwarranted angry outbursts. Self-regulation also makes it easier to put yourself in someone else's shoes which increases the odds of a positive emotional response as opposed to a careless reaction.

***Motivation****:*    Emotional    intelligence    and laziness don't mix. Motivation to succeed at personal goals, regardless of what those goals might be, is a primary drive for those with a high level of emotional intelligence. An increase in motivation can be beneficial in practically every aspect of your life and is a great way to give yourself the extra push you need, especially if you have found yourself in a bit of a slump recently.

***Empathy***: When it comes to your day to day interactions with others, empathy is hands-down one of the most valuable elements of emotional intelligence as a whole. While it is often confused with either compassion or sympathy, empathy is actually the ability to understand and relate to the emotions of another person. It directly relates back to withholding judgment, which is reinforced through self-regulation. Those who have a high degree of empathy can understand when others are feeling a specific way and respond according to their goals and desires.

For example, if someone is depressed because they didn't get a promotion, the empathy will try to cheer that person up and redirect them from the depressed state even if they don't much care one way or the other. Empathy is the difference between listening to what someone is saying and understanding what they are feeling.

***Social skills****:* Those with naturally high EQ are often leaders because they have a natural ability to connect with others, manage their emotions and inspire them in one way or another. This is often a natural result of the other elements of emotional intelligence, and it is possible the leader in question isn't even doing such things intentionally, their situation is just a result of their innate abilities.

## EQ versus IQ

First and foremost, EQ is not to be confused with IQ. IQ (Intelligence Quotient) comes from a series of standardized tests that measure the level of someone's academic and intellectual intelligence and ability. EQ (Emotional

Quotient), while it can be measured via testing, says more about how a person actually functions and interacts with other people.

You are born with your IQ whereas EQ is developed through your experiences. Think of your IQ as a set of parameters that dictate the extent of your cognitive abilities whereas EQ is the foundation which you are free to build upon through your personal experiences. It is essentially cognition versus intuition. EQ is how you can put your IQ to use. In other words, IQ is what you can do whereas EQ is how and/or why you do it.

While IQ was the standard for measuring a person's likelihood for success in the future for over a century, since the release of Goleman's book, EQ has become an increasingly valuable metric that companies look for in prospective employees. For example, an IQ test can determine a child's overall likely capability in the classroom, but it will provide little relevant information when it comes to determining how that child learns best, thinks critically or interacts with others.

Especially in the past decade, more and more corporations and businesses are ditching the IQ tests and opting for EQ assessments when hiring and placing potential employees. The results have been overwhelmingly in favor of EQ over IQ. In a study done by the Robert H. Smith School of Business (2016), 71% of hiring managers said that they value EQ over IQ when hiring and 59% said that would not hire someone with a high IQ but a low EQ.

## Understanding the basics of emotion

A core part of emotional intelligence is the ability to identify the emotions that another person is experiencing or to do the same for yourself to ensure you keep your emotions under control. The best way to do this is to understand the core human emotions and how to identify them in short order.

In the 1970s, a researcher by the name of Paul Eckman outlined six basic human emotions that have been hardwired into the human brain over countless generations. As such, these emotions are known to elicit the strongest and most instinctual responses out of all possible emotions. These include surprise, sadness, happiness, fear, disgust, and anger. These six emotions can be considered the buildings blocks upon which all other emotions are created.

*Components of emotions:* According to Mayer, an emotion occurs when there are certain biological, certain experiential, and certain cognitive states which all occur simultaneously. What this means is that the basic emotions all have three primary aspects including:

1. Subjective/cognitive experience; (The specific emotion we feel.)

2. Physiological response; (How the emotion manifests itself within us.)

3. Behavioral response; (The outward expression of the emotion.)

***Subjective/cognitive experience:*** While there are emotions that everyone, regardless of age, race or culture is going to experience, they are going to experience them subjectively based on those classifiers, as well as many more. Additionally, it is important to consider the many ways that a particular person could express a given emotion when it is pure, versus when it is mixed with other emotions instead. Some of these various types of responses are outlined below.

***Psychological response***: According to the Cannon-Bard Theory of Emotion, people experience emotion, as well as any relevant physiological responses to those emotions simultaneously. What this means is that if your hands sweat when you get nervous, then this physical response is triggered at the exact moment you start feeling the emotion in question. This occurs due to the way the sympathetic nervous system works, which itself is a subset of the autonomic system which controls various involuntary functions such as breathing. The sympathetic system is responsible for all of the body's flight or fight responses, along with the physical responses to emotion. The amygdala is responsible for the physical responses you feel to emotion as well as feelings of hunger and thirst as well. As such, a common reaction to trauma to the amygdala is a dramatically less extreme fear response.

***Behavioral response***: A behavior response is a way in which emotion is expressed as opposed to the physical response it generates. This includes things like smiling, frowning and other expressions of emotion. While some are universal, others require a degree of emotional intelligence to penetrate as many are cultural and what is perfectly acceptable in on country could be downright scandalous in another. With the appropriate level of emotional intelligence, you will be able to tell what the other party's emotional response to a given situation is, regardless of the physical signs they are giving off. When someone expresses an emotion, an emotionally intelligent person can not only identify that emotion but can interpret and respond to it based on the expression and/or body language.

# Chapter 2:
# Test Your Emotional Intelligence

To actually get started improving your emotional intelligence, it is important to understand where you are starting out from. Answer the following list of questions honestly and remember if you lie then the only person you are going to end up hurting is yourself. Once you have tallied up your answers, keeping reading for a breakdown of just what your score means.

When going over the following questions, it is important to be as honest with yourself as possible. There are no right answers here, just the most accurate answers to your specific scenario. Only by answering honestly will you be able to determine a baseline that you can successfully work from in the future.

**Very false** *answers are going to be worth 1 point*

**Somewhat false** *answers are going to be worth 2 points*

**Slightly correct** *statements are going to be worth 3 points*

**Mostly correct** *statements are going to be worth 4 points*

**Entirely correct** *statements are going to be worth 5 points*

**I always understand the things I am feeling when I am feeling them.**

*Very false*

*Somewhat false*

*Slightly correct*

*Mostly correct*

*Entirely correct*

**I find it easy to remain calm even when the situation that I find myself in becomes extremely frustrating.**

*Very false*
*Somewhat false*
*Slightly correct*
*Mostly correct*
*Entirely correct*

**Other people describe me as being a good listener.**

*Very false*
*Somewhat false*
*Slightly correct*
*Mostly correct*
*Entirely correct*

**When I am anxious or upset, it is easy for me to calm myself down.**

*Very false*
*Somewhat false*
*Slightly correct*
*Mostly correct*
*Entirely correct*

**Working with large groups is easy for me.**

*Very false*
*Somewhat false*
*Slightly correct*
*Mostly correct*
*Entirely correct*

**Focusing on long-term goals is easy for me to do.**

*Very false*
*Somewhat false*
*Slightly correct*

*Mostly correct*

*Entirely correct*

**When I have negative thoughts and feelings, I don't let them affect my day.**

*Very false*

*Somewhat false*

*Slightly correct*

*Mostly correct*

*Entirely correct*

**I know my weaknesses, as well as I, know my strengths.**

*Very false*

*Somewhat false*

*Slightly correct*

*Mostly correct*

*Entirely correct*

**I enjoy negotiations and defusing conflict.**

*Very false*

*Somewhat false*

*Slightly correct*

*Mostly correct*

*Entirely correct*

**I enjoy the work I do.**

*Very false*

*Somewhat false*

*Slightly correct*

*Mostly correct*

*Entirely correct*

**Constructive criticism is a useful tool that helps you to learn.**

*Very false*

*Somewhat false*

*Slightly correct*

*Mostly correct*

*Entirely correct*

**I regularly set long-term goals and then see them through.**

*Very false*
*Somewhat false*
*Slightly correct*
*Mostly correct*
*Entirely correct*

**I find it easy to understand the nonverbal cues that other people give off.**

*Very false*
*Somewhat false*
*Slightly correct*
*Mostly correct*
*Entirely correct*

**I enjoy making small talk.**

*Very false*
*Somewhat false*

Emotional Intelligence

*Slightly correct*
*Mostly correct*
*Entirely correct*

**I am an active listener.**

*Very false*
*Somewhat false*
*Slightly correct*
*Mostly correct*
*Entirely correct*

**Figure out your score**

Once you have answered the questions above, the next thing you are going to need to do is to figure out your score. Keep in mind that completely inaccurate statements are 1 point, somewhat inaccurate statements are worth 2 points, slightly accurate statements are worth 3 points, mostly accurate statements are worth 4 points, and always accurate statements are worth 5 points.

Chapter 2: Test Your Emotional Intelligence

***More than 14 points and less than 35 points***: If you scored within this range, then you are already on the right track when it comes to reading this book as you definitely need to work on your emotional intelligence. If you often feel overwhelmed when you need to deal with issues that are emotionally taxing or during stressful situations, then you are likely in this category. If you tend to naturally avoid emotional situations as you know, they are outside of your wheelhouse, or if you have a hard time calming yourself down after an emotional experience, then you are likely in this category as well.

If you scored in this range, then it is important to work on raising your emotional intelligence as much as possible, as quickly as possible, as you will only see improvements across the board as a result. While you are certainly on the right track, it is important to keep in mind that this is definitely going to be a difficult journey which means you are going to need to prepare for some hard work if you plan on moving forward successfully. It will also be a good idea to keep reminding yourself that you can improve your emotional intelligence with practice, which means it will only get easier with time. Never forget, the obstacles that you now find in your path are in no way insurmountable, keep putting one foot in front of the other, and you will find success sooner than you might expect.

***More than 34 and less and 56 points***: If you scored in this range then congratulations, you have an average amount of emotional intelligence. As such, you are likely able to get along alright in most situations, but you could use a bit of work if you want to stand out in this arena. If you find yourself in this category, then you are going to want to strive to learn more about emotional intelligence whenever and wherever you can while at the same time keeping up the good work you have already done. While this means you won't necessarily be learning something new every single day, you should always be working towards some long-range goal that will improve your emotional intelligence in the long run.

***More than 55 points:* If you scored more than 55 points** then you are already in the upper echelons of emotional intelligence. You are likely often described as charismatic or insightful, and those you meet might like you without knowing quite why. This doesn't mean there isn't still more you can do when it comes to ensuring your emotional intelligence skills are in tip-top shape, however, as there is always more to learn. If you don't know where to start, you may find that moving into a position of leadership at work could be rewarding. Regardless of what you do next, it is key that you don't get so caught up in the wants and needs of others that you don't sacrifice your own happiness for someone else's.

# Chapter 3:
# Start Small

After you have a good understanding of what emotional intelligence is all about, as well as the myriad of things that it can do for you and where your EQ is currently at, the next thing you are going to want to do is to get yourself used to the idea of improving in this fashion through some small starter exercises. Especially if your EQ is much lower than you would like, it is important to keep in mind that you won't be raising it to the mid-70s overnight which means it is best to start off with some simple practice to get into the swing of things.

First things first, you are going to want to practice the following at least twice a day, once in the morning and once at night to keep you in an emotionally intelligent mindset. When choosing the time to start your exercises, ensure that it is time you can easily repeat each day as your mind will take to the practice more easily with the added repetition. Finally, you will want to practice each and every day for a full month to ensure these exercises become full-blown habits.

*Take a closer look at your feelings:* If you are like most people these days, then you are likely to find it difficult to sort your day from the hectic mess of appointments and deadlines that you have to muddle through. As such, it can be difficult to correctly monitor your thoughts, much less your emotional state. This issue can then frequently be compounded even more by other stressors and distractions that can make it easy for poorly thought out actions to slip through which never do any good for anybody. This is why it is crucial that you get in the habit of practicing proper communication when you get a chance which means prioritizing communications with others when they do occur.

Emotions are often tied to events that take place in your immediate vicinity, but this doesn't automatically mean that they are valid. It is actually common for the emotion you are feeling right now, to be tied to something you have felt in the past that this situation is simply reminding you of. If you find yourself dealing with this type of scenario, then regardless of how you feel in the moment, it is likely that you are dealing with an incorrect response which means you will need to work on limiting that association in your mind ASAP. Learning to understand which emotions you are feeling at the moment, and why, is a crucial step to improving your EQ in the long-term.

Being aware of your feelings is a skill which means that it can be improved if you are willing to practice doing so. To that end, you should pick a set time each day to practice this skill, once in the morning and then again in the evening. When practicing, you are going to want to check-in with all of the emotions you have felt since your last check-in and determine if the emotion you felt was an accurate response to the stimuli that was taking place at the time. Ideally, you are going to want to remember moments of intense emotion for the best effect. When thinking back to these emotions, consider the physical response that it brought out in you as well as the mental response. Do your best to connect the feelings you have to a specific emotion so that you can become aware of what is going on when you feel it again in the future.

*Consider your behavior more closely:* After you are somewhat more comfortable keeping an eye on your mental state, the next thing you will need to do is get into the habit of paying attention to the way your emotions affect your actions and also which emotions and actions are most frequently associated with one another. You should be sure you consider this with both positive and negative emotions as this information is going to be useful for all emotions, not just those you are trying to avoid. The more you learn about the breadth of the emotional spectrum, the more easily you will be able to identify the emotions that others are feeling as well. As an added bonus, once you have cataloged the emotions for reference in the future, you will also find that it is much easier to understand when you are headed down an emotional path, so you can take a detour as needed.

When paying attention to the behaviors you most frequently experience, it is crucial that you don't muddle up the process by trying to pass judgment on the things you are feeling. Passing judgment on yourself is only going to add a more complex layer of emotions on top of everything that is already going on, making it more difficult to unravel successfully. Instead of judging yourself, you will find it more beneficial to make a concentrated effort to take note of the feelings and actions as you experience them, as well as how they affect those around you both in the moment and in the long-term. It is also important to pay attention to the ways it affects your ability to communicate, your productivity, and your overall level of satisfaction.

*Take responsibility for your emotions:* If you have a naturally low EQ, then it may be difficult to come to terms with the idea that you are directly responsible for your emotions. While it may be hard to grasp at first, the truth of the matter is that despite the fact that your emotion is generally a response to an external emotion, the truth is that you have more control in this situation than you might expect. With practice, you will learn to take responsibility for your feelings and, as such, all of the actions that you took while feeling those emotions as well.

As such, when you are first getting into the habit of improving your emotional intelligence, then you are going to want to set aside a bit of time each day to really think about this fact and consider its implications. You should treat it as a personal mantra, which means you are going to want to think about it morning, noon and night, and anywhere in between that, you get a chance. Eventually, it will be running through your head at all times, and you will be free to think of your feelings as a tool rather than something unpredictable that needs to be guarded. This is a crucial step when it comes to working to improve your EQ for the better.

*Respond in the best way possible:* When dealing with an emotionally charged situation at the moment, the most common way that most people react is to do the first thing that comes into their heads, without taking the time to think it through. Reacting is a type of automatic, unconscious response, which is why it and to snap judgments go so well together. On the other hand, responding to a situation, instead of reacting, allows you to make a rational, and well-reasoned response. While reacting may let off more emotional steam at the moment, the results are rarely going to as positive as they would have been if you had taken the time to respond appropriately instead.

To ensure you get into the habit of responding instead of reacting, you will need to take some time throughout the day to take a few extra moments when you find yourself in an emotionally charged situation. This will give you the extra time you need to ensure that what you think are responses aren't just reactions that you sat on for a few extra seconds. The best way to go about doing so is to consider why it is you feel the way you do before making a choice in question. You will also need to consider why you think the choice you are favoring is the best way to resolve the situation in question so that everyone is happy moving forward. Putting yourself in the shoes of anyone else involved is also a good choice as it will make it easier to empathize with them as well.

*Watch your values:* As you proceed through your daily routine, it is important to make a conscious effort to monitor the things you do and also consider why exactly it is that you are doing them. At the same time, stop to think if it is really the best use of your time at the current moment. If you realize you have made a mistake, don't waste time scolding yourself, simply dig deeper and figure out what you should be doing instead for the best results.

You may find that making a list of all of the things you do on a given day will help quite a bit when it comes to identifying the things that are most important to you. This will, in turn, make it easier to pinpoint how you should be spending your time when it comes to actively furthering these types of goals. Doing so will also allow you to focus more closely on the feelings you are experiencing, ultimately allowing you to know yourself more completely than may otherwise ever be the case. If you discover that you are doing many things for apparently the wrong reasons, then your best bet is to consider your core values as there is a good chance something, somewhere, is out of whack. If you take a closer look at your list, consider if anything has changed recently as this could be the related to the change.

While all of the above information at your fingertips, you should then be able to really work through whatever it is that has been going on in your life lately that would alter your emotions in such a way that they would realign in a way you don't approve of. If this happens to you, it is important to not get discouraged if you have a hard time connecting the cause and effect in this instance as it can be difficult to do without digging deeper. With enough hard work and dedication to the task at hand, however, you should be able to determine just what is going on and what emotional changes need to be made to get things back on track.

# Chapter 4:
# Improve Your Self-Awareness

Before you are able to start working on your emotional intelligence reliably, you need to focus on being as self-aware as possible. On this will allow you to figure out how to prepare for your most common reactions and understand where exactly it is that they come from? This is why this chapter is going to explore some of the topics of becoming more self-aware, including how to meditate and even writing down some of your big goals and priorities so you can finally have a plan in place.

*Meditation:* Meditation is one of the first habits you should pick up when it comes to increasing your emotional intelligence by becoming more self-aware. Meditation is useful in this sense as it allows you to take a break from whatever it is that is going on in the momentum from the emotions that you are currently feeling overwhelmed by. If you can find as little as 15 minutes per day, you will quickly learn how to detach yourself from the world which will lead to an increased ability to detach from the world by thinking about it objectively as a way that is ruled and defined by your emotions.

While there are certainly those who prefer a complicated setup, mediation doesn't have to be difficult. It will take some time to train your brain to avoid focusing on the negative and stressful things in your life, but with a little hard work and determination, you will start to see noticeable results in as little as a few weeks' time. If you are just getting started with meditation for the first time, don't worry, this practice is easy. All you need to do is pick out a room where you can be alone for a few minutes without interruption. Sit on the floor, unless you have issues with your back, in which case a chair is fine, as long as you sit up straight, with your hands in your lap.

Once you have gotten comfortable, you will want to close your eyes and focus on taking deep, even breaths. Most people breathe quite a bit faster than necessary, so it is important that you make a conscious effort to slow yours down as much as possible. Early on, it is perfectly normal for your mind to wander when you are trying to reach a meditative state. Don't let yourself get frustrated with this, as your mind is used to working at full speed to keep up with everything you normally have going on throughout the day, so it simply doesn't know how to take things slow.

As such, whenever you find yourself thinking about the activities of the day while meditating, all you need to do is gently remind yourself to focus on the task at hand and return to thinking about your breathing. This will likely be tough at first, but after a few sessions, you should be able to remain focused on the task at hand without any issues.

There are also numerous different types of mediation that you can work with, outside of the basic form discussed above. You may instead find that you like to repeat a specific word, sound or mantra, throughout your meditation to help you focus. Some people find it useful to listen to music at the same time, something orchestral and light. You may also find guided meditation to be a useful choice, at least at first, as having someone walk you through the process can make it a good deal easier overall.

Visualization is popular because you can focus on a picture in your head and pick what you want to concentrate on, rather than just concentrating on your own breathing. You can choose any of these methods that you would like as long as they help you to forget all the worries, troubles, and stresses of life and force you to concentrate on the here and now. It only takes about fifteen minutes a day, although you can choose to meditate for longer or do it a few times a day if you need too, and you will see a big difference. You will start to feel calmer in many situations, you will be able to notice when your triggers come around, and so much more.

Meditation is not the only technique that is useful when it comes to helping to calm down the brain and help it to be more self-aware. You may also find success with yoga, which allows you to work on your concentration while exercising at the same time. Visualization is also a great choice for those who have trouble only focusing on their breathing as it also more of a visual component to make it easier for you to relax. Getting a massage could also help you to improve your mindset as it will help you to get your breathing in line. You may also find success mixing and match some of the suggestions outlined above to see what works best for you.

## Self-Assess

To truly become more self-aware, you are going to need to start by rating yourself regarding your various weaknesses and strengths. If you discover that you are having a difficult time having an honest and open discussion with yourself about yourself, then you may want to ask others for help, as discussed below. You may also find it useful to take a variety of different personality tests and seeing where they overlap when it comes to rating your abilities, skills and personal values. Finally, if you are just having a hard time getting started, there are plenty of ways you can get your self-assessment juices flowing.

*Write it down:* When it comes to actively being more self-aware, you may want to try writing down your priorities, along with your short and long-term plans. You likely frequently have plans or goals floating around in your head, but rarely take the time to actually take the time to actually write them down. As such, when you get in the habit of doing so, you may very well be surprised at how much more concrete this process makes them and how much of a difference this makes when it comes to your overall self-awareness as well.

As such, the first step is going to be making a list of all the things you want to accomplish shortly, including specific plans and goals, before then deciding on the way to measure your progress along the way. You need to be as detailed as possible with this. For example, Warren Buffet is one person who is known for articulating the reasons that he makes an investment right when he makes that investment, rather than doing it at some point later. He has a lot of journal entries that work as a record to help him figure out whether the outcome of new investment was from luck or sound judgment.

Now, all of your future plans may not be on investments, but you can work with a similar approach. You can lay out the plans that you want to work on, such as getting a promotion or a new job at work, going on vacation, starting your own business or something else, but they write down the reasons that you want to accomplish these goals. The reasons should be well-thought out and sound but remember that no one else is reading them so if they seem a bit silly, don't worry about it.

The entire point of this exercise is to make it easier for you to think about your plans for the future in an active, rather than a passive, way. It is easy to feel frustrated if you feel as though you are stuck in one place at all times, and not reaching the goals you would like. When you start writing your goals down, however, along with the reasoning behind them, it makes it easy to see where real plans exist, as opposed to those where the goal is more of a dream that you are kind of hopping will work out on its own.

With this realization laying your poorly outlined plans bare, it can then be far easier to change up your game plan and try something different. In fact, you will often find a significant improvement from just coming up with the plans it will give you something to look forward to and also work towards which can ensure you have a much better overall outlook as a result.

When following through on this practice, it is important you go with a physical journal and that you get in the habit of writing in it every night. Keep a running tally of experiences, how they made you feel and the physical reactions that came along with them. Make sure you take note of physical expressions of the emotions including sore shoulders, stiff neck or an increased heart rate. While you might find it difficult to keep track of all the different emotional experiences you had throughout the day at first, it is important to keep at it as it will help you be more naturally aware of your inner state in the long run.

From there, you will want to expand on your list to include the part you played specifically. After you have already gotten into the habit of listing your daily emotional experiences, you can then start adding in the role you played during each of the moments you are keeping track of. Roles include things like father, employee, sister, spectator, etc. keep the roles relatively broad as you will want there to be enough overlap between days that after a while you can start to notice a pattern. Ideally, this will reveal what types of roles you are the most comfortable in as well as those to avoid or strengthen if the response is perceived as a weakness.

From there, you will be able to more easily use the journal as a roadmap when moving forward as it will allow you to more easily associate specific emotions with specific roles. This, in turn, will make it easier for you to control your emotions as you will know what to expect. Forewarned is forearmed, so when you know that you will be going into a situation with negative emotional connotations because you have been there before, you can take a moment to prepare yourself for the experience in hopes of making it through as unscathed as possible.

Much like having a physical journal to write in, it is crucial that you work to isolate each emotion you believe you are about to feel so that it can be felt as clearly as possible. Likewise, you will want to name off the emotions you are about to feel for the best results; names have power and by name your emotions you are more likely to tame them. Once you are aware of potential emotions, you can prevent negative reactions from being on guard for them. With enough practice, your defenses for such negative response will naturally activate at the sign of emotional trouble and get in the habit of preparing for them will make these defenses as formidable as possible.

*Get feedback from those around you:* Many people feel the urge to run from feedback as they believe that any type of criticism they receive is inherently negative and without true value in one way or another. Unfortunately for these individuals, this belief structure is causing them to miss out on an opportunity to learn more about themselves and the areas that they could improve upon if only they were aware of the issue. If this sounds like you, then the sooner you start to understand that this feedback can be used as a means of bettering yourself, then the sooner you will be able to sit back and listen to the things people are trying to help you with.

There are plenty of different ways you can start receiving constructive feedback, starting with asking your family and friends to give it to you straight. This is a great place to start if you have a fear of this sort of honesty as these are the people you know best. Which means they have likely noticed plenty about you over the years that you could improve on, and will also have the compassion to explain the situation to you in such a way that it won't hurt your feelings more than necessary.

To get started with this exercise, the first thing you are going to want to do is to talk with those you are closest to and express your sincere desire that they express their true thoughts and opinions about you and the way you present yourself. Before they start, it is important that they feel they can safely assess you without consequence, and truly understand that you won't feel attacked or get defensive when they say something you don't agree with. There is likely going to be some negative feedback at this stage, and it is important that you accept this fact and understand that it is crucial so that you can ultimately move forward productively and make changes that benefit you not just in the short-term but in the long-term as well.

Remember, the goal of this exercise is to get as much direct and honest feedback as possible which means that you are going to want to avoid responding to what is said and only soak it in instead. Once you know what it is you need to work on, you can then ask these same individuals to call you out when you are behaving in a way that you want to change. This can work either with issues that have just been called to light or those that have been exposed previously, anything that can be observed by others is fair game.

For example, if you have a bad habit of always having to be the center of attention, you can have your friends let you know when this is starting to be an issue, and thus nip the problem in the bud as a result. Make it clear that they are really doing you a favor, however, as this will ensure that they are more likely to help you out as opposed to staying quiet in hopes of not hurting your feelings.

Once you have gotten used to receiving feedback from your friends and family, you will then want to move on to the workplace as well. Typically, many companies will have some sort of feedback program in place already either through human resources or through management. As long as this process is done in a productive, respectful way, it can give you a good idea of what strengths and weakness you are dealing with professionals.

While hearing so much feedback all at once can be difficult to deal with, especially if you previously preferred to avoid it entirely, it is a critical part of becoming more self-aware in the short-term and increases your emotional intelligence in the long-term. It is easy to get stuck in the same old routine to the point that you don't even actively think about all the things you are doing each day or how your actions cause others to view you. Taking the first step of asking for feedback and working to ensure the changes stick is a crucial part of improving your EQ once and for all.

# Chapter 5:
# The Power of Expression

In order to truly improve your emotional intelligence, not just in theory but in practice, you are going to need to ensure you can express yourself effectively, even when it might not be easy to do so. Unfortunately, this is often easier said than done as it can often be a much more straightforward task to simply stay quiet and go along with the group, doing things you may not strictly enjoy rather than taking a risk that may disturb the group dynamics and cause people to think less of you. While this might work for a short time, it is really only putting a band-aid on the issue and forcing you to feel even worse in the process.

Emotional Intelligence

In this chapter, you will learn all about expressing yourself in healthy, productive ways. It is important to keep in mind that fully expressing yourself is no excuse for making other people feel bad or harm others in any way unless this harm is unavoidable and serves the greater good. Keep in mind, emotional intelligence is about more than just listening and understanding the feelings of others, it is also about expressing yourself as clearly as possible when it comes to your feelings, emotions, and thoughts, as well as the intersection of the three. Keep the following in mind when it comes to expressing yourself as effectively as possible.

*Only worry about impressing yourself:* While you may feel as though it is nice to be respected, the truth of the matter is that, by and large, it rarely matters what other people think of you. While this seems to fly in the face of everything the modern world of social media stands for, it's true, the only opinion that you need to worry about is your own. No matter how hard you work, some people are going to talk about you behind your back, some will get angry with what you are trying to do and still, other's will make fun of you. The only good news here is that this will always be a small minority of people, which means it is rarely as big of a deal as they would lead you to believe.

When it comes to expressing yourself freely, one of the first things you will need to keep in mind is the fact that, no matter how embarrassing or important an action you take is to you, there is a better than average chance that no one else will even remember it in the morning. One of the most difficult parts of expressing themselves successfully that most people have trouble getting past is the idea that people are going to judge them harshly for expressing themselves in an unguarded way. The truth of the matter is that most people are so absorbed with whatever is going on in their own lives that they likely won't think twice about what you have to say and even if they do notice they are unlikely to believe it is nearly as big of a deal as you do.

While the thought that those around you are rarely giving you, their undivided attention isn't great, it should still be a liberating realization overall. Spending all of your time worrying about what others think about you can be exhausting and more than enough to put anyone on edge. Moving forward, rather than worrying about how everyone around you is going to react to your actions, focus on taking actions that you can feel good about after the fact and let everyone else take care of themselves.

As long as you believe you can stand behind your actions after the fact, regardless of what others might think about them, them go ahead and move forward, you really have very little to lose. However, if you feel the action you are considering might leave you feeling ashamed of what you are doing, then you may be better off just picking another course instead. With everything that you do in life, concentrate on impressing yourself, and you will honestly start impressing other people in the process.

*Aim to stand for something:* How many people do you know that always seem to be a little bit lost or confused? They always go along with whatever the crowd wants to do and never really gives a concrete thought or opinion of their own. They may appear happy on the surface, but underneath they likely feel resentful as they are unable to speak up for themselves, even when it is very important they do so. This resent often leads to an against the world mentality that can be extremely harmful when it comes to improving your emotional intelligence.

If you are one of those people who always tend to follow the crowd, then odds are you need to learn to stand for something. The line you draw in the sand doesn't need to be major, it just needs to be something that you legitimately care about. For example, if you are with a group of friends who are considering where they want to go for dinner, if you don't like Thai food, and someone suggests Thai food, speak up for yourself and register your displeasure. It is unlikely that anyone is going to get offended by your announcement; on the contrary, they will take your statement into consideration, and you may not have to suffer through an hour at a place that has nothing you want to eat.

This is a relatively innocuous example that, when practiced regularly, will make it far easier to get into the habit of speaking up for yourself than you otherwise might. In fact, much of the frustration that comes along with modern life actually occurs because people are too worried about angering those around them which causes them to remain quiet to their own detriment. Unfortunately, when you live your life constantly worrying about what others will think of you, you will end up repressed, angry, stressed and with a lower overall level of emotional intelligence than you may otherwise have.

This is only true to a point, however, as obviously if the things you want to do involve causing physical or emotional harm to another person you are going to want to think twice instead. You will still need to be empathetic, of course, but there is a fine line between being empathetic and being a doormat. The key is to learn when speaking up and stating your opinion is the right choice and when it is better to listen to what others have to say in hopes of reaching a compromise and learning the difference is a key part of improving your EQ.

*Find your muse:* You may find that expressing yourself comes more naturally to you if you can find a muse that brings the self-expression out of you. While some people are going to be great at expressing themselves verbally, this does not make it the best, or most natural, form of expression for everyone.

As previously discussed, some people are naturally shy and have trouble speaking up, even when they have a perfectly valid reason for doing so, while others might just not like other people

# Chapter 5: The Power of Expression

or tend to trip over their tongue, even if they like to talk. Luckily there isn't just one way to effectively express yourself which means if talking is not your strong suit then the best thing you can do is get out there and find a method that works more naturally for you.

As such, the question you should be asking yourself is what your muse will be. For some, they may like the idea of organized public speaking, they may enjoy taking on a leadership role in the opportunities it forces them to speak to the public while also meeting new people. Other people may find that they can express themselves more clearly through their writing. While they may not be comfortable getting up to speak in front of a large crowd, they still have a way for words. These individuals may find journaling a useful way to get their thoughts out into the world where they can do the most good.

Emotional Intelligence

If you are naturally drawn to music, then maybe that is your muse instead. Playing music for yourself can help you work through complicated emotions and playing with others can help you get used to spending more time with other people while also giving you a way to interact directly with their emotions as well through the music.

The point is, your hobby can be anything that you are passionate about. As long as it allows you to be free and truly stop caring what others say or think about you, then you can call an activity your muse. Spending time on something you truly enjoy will allow you to show your true personality which also makes it easier for you to keep your emotions in check while also letting out the frustration that often makes it difficult to fully exercise your emotional intelligence.

# Chapter 6:
# Follow Your Passion

Finding your passion is a crucial part of improving your emotional intelligence in the long-term that will also allow you to discover the real, unique, you if you let it. Passion is another causality of modern life. Thanks to the constant stream of content that is available 24/7, there are always places to look that reflect the idea that you aren't good enough, qualified enough, special enough, to reach the brass ring. This, in turn, makes it easy to put off pursuing your passion in hopes of getting back to it after reaching this presumably attainable goal that nevertheless remains constantly out of reach.

Perhaps unsurprisingly, constantly striving for something that you can never have adds a lot of stress to the mix which is bad for people of all types, but proves especially stressful for those who are currently hard at work on improving their overall EQ. This chapter will walk you through the process of rediscovering your passions and even some tips on how to slow down a bit so that the body and the brain have some time to relax and not feel so overworked all the time.

*Stop and take a breath:* When it comes to improving your overall emotional intelligence, one of the most important things you can do is to learn to slow down. The best way to do so is to finally come to terms with the fact that, no matter how hard you work, you won't be able to please everyone all of the time. For those who are naturally inclined to help others, the idea of saying no to someone else can make them physically ill. It is literally one of the hardest things they will ever have to do because they cannot stomach the thought of feeling as though they failed someone else in any way.

While this type of thinking is certainly admirable, if it applies to you then you need to stop before you hurt yourself. After all, you are only one person and trying to do the work of two, or more, people are only going to harm you in the long run. After all, the candle that burns at both ends burns out twice as fast. This will lead you to a scenario where you never have time to think things through, much less relax properly, which is a rough state to be in if you hope to actively improve your emotional intelligence.

While it may be difficult to slow down and take things a little easier, especially at first, it is critical that you do so if you hope to stand a chance when working on your emotional intelligence. If you make more of a concentrated effort to slow down, you also make it easier to find the best version of yourself now that you have the time to start asking questions about just what that is exactly.

When it comes to slowing down in the long-term, there are several good places to start. While you are obviously still going to have tasks that definitively require your attention, you will find that even if you set aside just 15 minutes a day to yourself, it will make all the difference in the world. It is important to ensure that this time is at the same time each day and that it is a part of your routine, no matter what. You can use that time to practice yoga, meditate, go for a walk or simply sit in your favorite chair and clear your head for 15 minutes, anything that allows you to slow down and more thoroughly appreciate all that life has to offer.

While you will likely find it hard to calm yourself down and relax at first, it is important to keep it up as doing so is important to the long-term health of the mind and to ensure that your critical thinking skills remain sharp. Stress, which is often present can really cloud your judgment and can cause you to react in ways that you are not proud of. But if you learn to take it down a few notches and relax, you can think more clearly and get along with others better than ever before.

*Embrace what keeps you unique:* Everyone has something that sets them apart from the crowd and makes them unique. It is important to take the time to focus on what makes you unique and how you can best share your uniqueness with the world as opposed to focusing on the talents that others have that you do not. Embracing your uniqueness is another way of improving self-awareness and the power of self-expression while at the same time following your passion which means it is a great goal to add to your plan for improving your emotional intelligence.

If you spend all of your time bemoaning the fact that you are not as talented as another person in a specific way, especially if this person is someone you interact with regularly, then this is going to cause significant internal strife that will make it difficult for you to take positive steps at the same time. Letting go of unfounded feelings of envy will help you to feel more relaxed and ready to face the world than ever before, with a clear head on your shoulders to boot.

*Become more confident:* Building self-confidence is a dream that many people have, yet it is something that few actually pursue. This is because, like anything worth doing, getting started building self-confidence can be quite difficult especially if you have very little of it, to begin with. Unfortunately, without a reasonable amount of self-confidence, you won't be able to express yourself in a way that will legitimately improve your EQ in either the short or the long-term. Regardless of your current level of self-confidence, however, there are some simple yet productive thought exercises you can practice forcing your mind into the habit of thinking about things in the proper self-confident light.

When it comes time to assert yourself, if you find yourself becoming afraid, instead, you must first force yourself to understand that the only way this particular fear will ever leave you is if you master it completely. If you are uncertain about the outcome of a particular event, that uncertainty can manifest itself as anticipation which is just a hair's breadth from fear. Reacting in a scenario that would benefit from self-confidence with anxiety instead, will destroy any momentum that you may have previously developed.

As such, you may find it helpful to react to your anxiety as if it were actually curiosity. Instead of being anxious about an outcome you can instead trick your mind into being curious as to the results instead. Curiosity and self-confidence go together much more easily than anxiety and self-confidence, and you may find that curiously helps your confident momentum continue.

If you find yourself always responding to situations that require self-confidence in the same fearful pattern. Consider this, the human mind loves to find patterns, even when no true pattern exists. This means you may be responding to an established pattern and not actually the specifics of the current situation.

The next time you begin to feel scared or nervous before having to exhibit self-confidence, take the extra moment to consider your current situation and see what it is that is really making you feel that way. If nothing specific presents itself, then the odds are good that your mind is instead reacting to a pattern that doesn't really exist. With practice, you will find that you are able to improve your self-confidence and then use that newfound ability to improve your emotional intelligence as a result.

*Have more fun:* Life gets busy, especially as you get older, and before you know it you spend most days working to pay the bills and most of your days off running errands that you can't get to while you are working. What's more, this routine often develops in such a way that you don't realize the extent of the issue until you are buried up to your eyeballs in tasks with no end in sight. Focusing on these details leads to a myopic viewpoint that does little to improve your emotional intelligence in any way, shape, or form.

While it might seem silly, a great way to destroy that destructive viewpoint is to make a point of adding more fun to your life. As without fun, you will find that it is much more difficult to have a positive outlook on life, which in turn means thinking rationally when it comes to dealing with other people. While it may not seem like it now, it is possible to have a balance between your work and home life. What this balance means is going to be different for everyone, but even moving as little as 10 percent in a positive direction can have serious repercussions throughout your life. Focusing only on the things you get done from day to day can make it easy to feel bitter about all the things you are missing out on. When you take the time to focus on the fun that is already in your life, things can start seeming brighter almost immediately.

# Chapter 7:
# Self-Management

Once you have a clear understanding of yourself and the ways you can jump-start the improvement of your emotional intelligence, the first step to actively putting it to use in the real world is applying what you have learned in a real-world context. While you can easily start off having every intention of putting the things you have practiced into action, the stresses and pressures of the real world can make actually following through more difficult than you might expect. In order to ensure that applying your improving EQ becomes a habit, you need to use it every time you come up against emotional stress in any of its forms. Being angry is easy, being the right amount of anger about the situation in question takes far more work but is also far more rewarding in the long run.

Luckily, after you have worked through the exercises in the previous chapters, you should already notice that you are having an easier time when it comes to analyzing your emotions and thus responding rather than reacting. Hopefully, by studying the list of emotions, you often exhibit in given scenarios you will also be coming to understand that there is a time and a place for everything while also creating habits that relate to the proper response to emotions both positive and negative. The following habits can help you reinforce this new habit even more.

*Take time to consider your mentality:* Managing the emotions you feel in the moment effectively is all about putting away any victim mentality that you might have and instead enforcing a mentality that allows you to take full control of your emotions as well as the response that form as a result. Before you had taken the time required to properly index and understand your emotions along with their related physical responses, you could be forgiven for thinking the things that you did in the heat of the moment were the result of overpowering emotions, but that is all in the past. If you are strong enough to no longer be caught off guard by your emotions, then you can safely put this mentality away.

Changing your general outlook regarding what you think about your emotions will ultimately prime you to take charge at the moment when it matters most. Take a moment, right now, to make a commitment to yourself that you will no longer be a slave to your emotions.

*Cognitive reframing:* If you ever hope to manage your emotions effectively, you need to be able to manage your thoughts as well. Doing so means being able to interact with your negative thoughts so you can dismiss them, without having to worry about giving in to them in the interim. If you find yourself in a scenario where you feel your negative thoughts rolling in, try the following to determine if they are valid or not.

- Consider if the emotion that is welling up is related to a thought or idea that is reasonable or plausible. Often, especially in negative situations, the human brain likes to extrapolate potential outcomes based on the unreasonable information. While the negative response you might have to the emotion is rarely useful, using the emotion as an earmark as to whether the thought is valid can help you cut through exaggerated negative thoughts and emotions.

- If, after careful consideration, you find that the situation you find yourself in does, in fact, warrant a negative emotion, then the next thing you are going to want to do is to find any possible silver lining, no matter how spacious it might be. With this done, you will want to focus on that silver lining with as much strength and conviction you can muster. While it may seem like a little thing, this simple change in perspective can be enough to modify your emotions and therefore your thoughts far enough in a positive direction to make a real difference when it comes to seeing results.

- Upon closer consideration, you could also end up using the negative situation as a means for self-improvement. When a negative situation arises, rather than letting the negative emotion run its course, a more productive alternative is to instead reframe it with the ultimate goal of personal reflection or self-improvement instead. For example, if you were passed over for a promotion at work, you could get angry, sad or frustrated that the higher-ups were so blind as to pick someone besides you for the job.

However, a more productive strategy would instead be to take a look at the successful candidate's qualifications or simply ask and see why it was that you were passed over for the position. Taking the time to use the potentially negative motivational event as a means to better yourself for future endeavors takes the negative and turns it into a positive. Not only that but giving yourself a new goal will take the focus off the failure and make it easier to move past as well.

*Get physical with your stress:* If you find yourself regularly getting stressed out either as a result of a wide variety of different negative emotions or because you know an emotionally charged situation is forthcoming. Luckily, there are several different techniques you can practice helping keep your stress to a minimum, allowing you to respond to an emotional situation in the right way as a result.

- You can start by simply taking several long, deep breaths in a controlled fashion. This is an old but good for a reason, and if you have never tried it, then you may be surprised at how effective it can be at the moment. The reasoning here is that the average person typically breaths quite shallowly, especially when they are anxious. This, in turn, leads to a deoxygenated state which in turn causes a very real boost when it comes to the stress experienced during hectic situations. If you find yourself taking rapid, shallow breaths; instead, make a concentrated effort to expand your diaphragm as much as possible, filling your lungs completely with each cycle of breath.

- Next, you are going to want to make a concentrated effort to relax your muscles. When you find yourself in a stressful situation, your muscles naturally tense up. As such, if you start by focusing on relaxing these muscles, then it helps to calm you down as a result of your body naturally thinking the issue has been dealt with. While you are focusing on relaxing your muscles and breathing deeply, go through the rest of the exercises on this list for 10 seconds each.

- Start by raising your eyebrows, next close your eyes tightly, next slowly open your mouth as wide as possible before closing it again slowly. Next, hold each arm straight out in front of you and then form a tight fist, next, shrug your shoulders, then tense your biceps. Up next you should stand on the tips of your toes, tighten your abdominal muscles and finally curl your toes. Repeat as needed.

**Practice being mindful**

While the benefits of meditation have already been broadly discussed, when it comes to self-management, there are few better ways to jump-start the process than with mindfulness meditation. What's more, after you get the basics down you can practice it virtually anywhere. Mindfulness meditation is a type of meditation that encourages practitioners to exist as completely at the moment as much as possible while keeping their minds free of all thought. A major part of this is aware of thoughts without interacting with them, something that everyone who is looking to improve their EQ can benefit from. That's not all that mindfulness meditation is good for, in fact, studies show that those who practice being mindful for as little as 15 minutes per day are typically more relaxed and have a stronger sense of self.

What's more, regularly practicing mindfulness is known to improve the attention span, increase body awareness and improve information retention. It is also known to physically improve brain health by making it possible for the brain to retain a greater amount of volume throughout the aging process while also thickening the hippocampus which makes learning new and complex topics, such as increasing your EQ, easier than it might otherwise be. Finally, it has been shown to decrease activity in the amygdala which generates stress, fear, and anxiety.

Mindfulness is also helpful for those who are looking to improve their emotional intelligence as being mindful has also been proven to enhance verbal reasoning skills while also decreasing the amount of cortisol, the primary hormone responsible for stress, which is found in the body. It should also make it easier for you to be self-aware and to track all of the various emotions that you feel throughout the day.

*Getting started:* When you first start practicing mindfulness, it is important to always practice at the same day to ensure your body is going to get into the habit of entering a mindful state each and every day, to make the transition easier to manage. Don't forget, it takes about a month for a new habit to solidify in your mind which means that as long as you can keep it up for that amount of time, you can keep it up indefinitely.

To reach a state of mindfulness, you are going to want to find someplace comfortable, and quiet to sit, though not so quiet and comfortable that you are tempted to fall asleep. Then, all you need to do is breathe deeply, in and out. As you breathe in, focus all of your attention on the information that your senses are providing to you, focus on the way the air feels in your lungs, how it smells and how it tastes. Slowly but surely, expand your consciousness so that you are taking in as much information about your surroundings as possible.

When you can reach a point where you are thinking about nothing except what is happening right now, then you have experienced a state of mindfulness. If you find yourself having a hard time reaching that point, you may have success picturing yourself staring at a stream of bubbles flowing by, each one representing a thought. If you find yourself being drawn into to interacting with a specific thought, simply visualize it floating away instead.

*Commute mindfully:* By practicing mindfulness meditation on the road, you will find that you often arrive at work ready to meet the challenges of the day head on and return home each night with a clear heart and head, the cares of the day forgotten on the highway. Practicing mindfulness meditation on the go will allow you to reach your destination in a focused, calm state that further allows the stresses of rush hour traffic fade into the background. Even better, practicing mindfulness on the go will help you stay completely focused at the moment and thus on the traffic that surrounds you.

To make the most of your commute in this fashion, you are going to want to begin practicing mindfulness starting from the very first moment you first get in the vehicle. This means you will need to begin by announcing your intention to the universe aloud, so you can actively work at getting into the right mindset. Once your intentions have been made plain, the next thing you will want to do is to take several deep, relaxing breaths, focusing on the sensations that your senses are providing you at the same time. This should help you find a mindful mindset before you even hit the road.

At the same time, you are going to want to take the time to focus on your body and the way it feels as you sit behind the wheel. Consider the way your hands feel on the steering wheel and the way the world around you looks as you stare out at it from behind your windshield. From there, let the sensations of feeling expand ever outward and downward so that you feel your feet and the pressure you exert on the pedals before starting your vehicle.

As you begin your commute you are going to want to pay special attention to everything that is going on around you, both to the vehicles that you are directly interacting with as well as the people on the sidewalk and the buildings and signs that you previously passed without giving them a second thought. While this is going on be sure to also give some attention to your eyes as they are taking everything in and your ears as they convey the sounds of hundreds, if not thousands, of other people all moving together in relative harmony. Focus on these things, and only these things while you drive, and you will be surprised at how much less of a hassle waiting in traffic suddenly becomes.

While this might initially strike you as too simple to produce the type of results you are looking for, it is important to put your doubts aside and give it a try before writing it off completely. Remember, when you first get started, even if you have already begun practicing mindfulness meditation in other facets of your life, it is perfectly natural for a stream of thoughts to be running through your head. This is especially true when heading to work as there are likely more things that you need to do than there are hours in the day to do them. Nevertheless, it is important to put everything else aside and strive to remain in the moment as thoroughly as possible.

# Chapter 8:
# Relationship Management

After you become more comfortable monitoring your actions and controlling the way you respond to external variables, it is finally time to start working on expanding your emotional intelligence, so you can successfully manage the emotions of those around you. In order to improve your social awareness, you need to start by focusing on improving your empathy while also ratcheting up the way you relate to the needs, emotions, and concerns of others.

Improving your empathy is a two-step process that involves both understanding what the other person is feeling and also making that other person feel as though you are both active participants in any conversation you may be having. While being more empathetic to those around you might seem relatively straightforward, studies show that this is a skill that society has a whole has gotten worse at, in direct correlation to the increase in popularity of electronic devices that are attached to screens. While society as a whole might be more connected than ever these days when placed face to face it is getting more and more difficult for people to relate to one another in person.

This, in turn, also makes it more difficult for people to trust one another, which can create an even greater gulf when it comes to feelings of personal isolation. As such, the best way to break out of this negative cycle is to go out of your way to respond positively to those around you when they come to you to express their thoughts and feelings. This will cause them to feel an even greater sense of trust towards you, which will help you to both feel less isolated and make additional empathetic gestures easier to come by in the future.

*Act more interested in whatever is going on:* The way that you present yourself during a conversation is just as important as what you say or what the conversation accomplishes. Being socially aware means making the extra effort to show the other person that you value their time and the conversation you are having. Consider your common interactions and think about how you appear to others. Consider if you take the time to put aside other distractions while speaking, make a point of making eye contact and generally listen in an active way instead of a passive one? Do you take the time to get input from others when it comes to how they feel about the topics covered in the conversation in question?

Think about these questions and make sure to always use open body language to convey to the other person that you are interested in what they have to say. Open body language includes leaning forward, arms that are not crossed, plenty of eye contact and smiling or laughing while not touch the face or creating artificial barriers. Ensure your body language matches your words and gauge the other person for the same for signs they are not comfortable in the current situation.

Ensuring that you are communicating effectively means taking the extra time to ensure that the messages you are sending are both clear and to the point and also ensuring that the other person is responding positively before moving on. Many people feel afraid to double check facts and specifics at the end of a long conversation for fear that it will make it seem as though they are not actively paying attention. The fact of the matter is the opposite is true, reiterating important facts at the end of a conversation gives the other party the impression that you were truly paying attention and want to ensure that everyone is on the same page before the conversation is over.

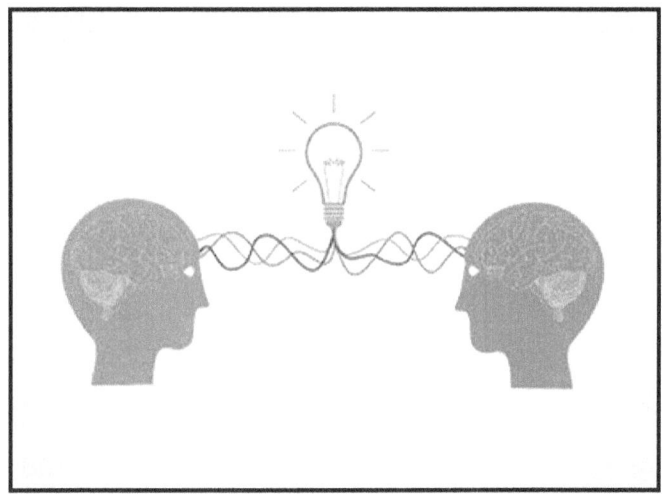

*Gauge the emotional response of others:* By this point, you should have a catalog of information at your fingertips when it comes to various emotional reactions which means that you should already be well on your way to figuring how other people fit into this framework as well. You can then move forward from there, extrapolating what other response and reactions are likely to be like when you find yourself in a specific situation. Being able to accurately predict what others are likely to say, think and do will also make it easier for you to respond in a way that is more likely to diffuse a situation.

To do so, all you need to try is thinking to yourself how you would diffuse the emotion if you were dealing with it yourself. Putting yourself in the other person's shoes is a great way to gauge their emotions and try and create a scenario where everyone walks away happy. You might not always gauge the other person's emotions perfectly, but either way, you will have more information for next time.

Be prepared for failure. Especially if you have a long way to go to get your EQ to where it needs to be, it is important to brace yourself for failure as it is likely you will misread a few physical signs of specific emotion because different people respond to the same stimuli in different ways. It is important that you understand these failures as a vital part of improving your social awareness as there are too many variations on common emotional response to ever learn them all by simply studying.

*Manage relationships effectively:* The ultimate culmination of all of your hard work at improving your emotional intelligence is learning to improve your relationship management skills to the point that you can be sure to control your emotions while also remaining aware of the emotional cues of those around you and keeping everything balanced at the same time. To get started successfully, the first thing you are going to need to do is to ensure you have a clear understanding of how you are affecting the other party, how they are affecting you and how any external forces are affecting you both. Only by having a strong understanding of all three will you be able to really find the best situation for everyone involved.

Once you have a clear view of the situation, you will then be able to come up with a decision that as to best proceed moving forward while still accounting for all the various moving pieces currently in play. While it will likely take your time to work your way through various possible outcomes, at first, with practice doing so will become a habit that barely warrants thinking twice about.

After you have come to the best decision possible, given the options you have to work well, you will also need to interact with the other parties in such a way that it is clear to them that you are working to understand their side of things and are looking to resolve things in a mutually productive way. It is important to not jump to attempting to juggle the emotional state of multiple individuals all at once, as they are all likely going to want different things and trying to please everyone, all at once, can lead to you helping no one instead. Rather, your best bet is going to be starting with just one other person and perfecting your one on one approach before moving on to groups. Regardless of how many people you are talking to, your goal should be to remain as empathetic as possible so that it is clear that you only want what is best for everyone involved.

When it comes to managing relationships successfully, your primary goal should be to ensure that every dispute you find yourself in leads to the outcome you want. This isn't a green light to only focus on your own needs at the expense of others, as this is a surefire way to create negative relationships in the long-term assuming your true goals ultimately come to light. Instead, your best bet is going to be to strive for outcomes that do the most good, regardless of who might come out ahead in any given situation. Managing relationships is a game of giving and take and navigating towards a minor setback now, could lead to greater concessions on the part of the other person at a later date. Keep the big picture in mind when it comes to making decisions, and you will always end up with the best results in the long term.

*Improving relationships:* When improving your relationships, it is important to think of the process as a journey rather than a destination. As such, you will never be at a point where all of your relationships require no additional effort to maintain or stabilize, but that isn't a bad thing. Relationships are living things which means they need regular care and attention to ensure they don't atrophy completely. Before you get started, it is crucial that you are confident in your ability to manage your own emotions as letting others draw you into a scenario where you think without acting is one of the worst ways to ruin a relationship.

## Chapter 8: Relationship Management

If you need to make a concentrated effort when it comes to improving or repairing a specific relationship, it is important to always do so with a firm plan in mind as going in without a plan is how you ended up in the current situation in the first place. This means you are going to need to start out by assessing the emotions of the other party as being aware will make it easier for you to determine any changes at the moment so that you can alter your plan accordingly.

When it comes to ensuring that you are ready to effectively manage the relationships in your life, it is also important to understand the best ways to persuade or influence those around you to see your side of things. You should also aim to inspire the other party to believe in a shared goal, help out with clearly productive feedback and genuinely constructive criticism; it is important to only use these last two if you know you can pull them off without sounding patronizing or passive aggressive as either is sure to make the situation worse. Finally, it is also important to consider how you can be the catalyst for change in the current scenario by managing conflict effectively through support and collaboration. You also need to focus on being a catalyst for change, manage conflict effectively and support teamwork and collaboration. If that seems like a whole lot of work, the following tips can help get you started.

- Take a look at the competencies listed above and decide how effective you are at each of them. Make a list of those that you are already competent at, being as detailed as possible.

- Next, to your list of strengths, write down the competencies that you are least sure of. Be as specific when it comes to your shortcomings as possible, if what you have written doesn't clearly lend itself to a specific path to improvement then you need to try again.

- Once you have a clear list in mind, the next thing you are going to want to do is to write down a number of clear, concrete action you can take to improve the areas that you need the most help with. From there, all that is left is to pick the area that you are going to work on first and get started. It is important to remember that you don't need to be amazing at all of the competencies right off the bat, as long as you are decent at each then you can learn and improve with practice.

# Chapter 9:
# Emotional Intelligence
# in the Workplace

Once you have improved your emotional intelligence to the point that you can successfully manage your own emotions and those of the people around you. You will have reached the most refined type of emotional intelligence possible, and it will have provided you with the ability to fully understand the perspective of another, even if it contradicts your own emotional state. Research has shown women, who traditionally rate higher on tests of emotional intelligence, tend to have a more collaborative and inclusive leadership style than men. Practiced by persons of any gender, emotional intelligence has much to offer the modern workplace and stakeholders across all functions:

- It makes it easier for leaders to motivate their employees because it helps them understand everyone's motivations.

- It helps to jumpstart collaboration while at the same time avoiding the pitfalls of groupthink.

- It makes it easier for leaders to determine and act on opportunities others might have missed.

- It aids in conflict resolution and ensures that issues are handled in a fair and evenhanded way.

- It has been proven to produce higher morale in employees and aid them in reaching their full potential.

## Chapter 9: Emotional Intelligence in the Workplace

*EQ in the hiring process:* While technical skills can be taught, it can be far more difficult to teach new hires the importance of emotional intelligence if they aren't already in the know. As such, it is often better to integrate concepts related to emotional intelligence into their hiring and professional development instead. As an example, it is far easier to prioritize testing for EQ at the entry-level position and then again when promoting from inside, rather than trying to teach these individuals things that will fundamentally alter core parts of their personality after the fact. While it will be work up front, you will always find that stakeholders with high EQ are more likely to have leadership potential themselves, leaving them the better choice, in the long run, every time.

While every role in a company is sure to benefit from a high degree of emotional intelligence in one way or another, not all are going to require a highly develop EQ to succeed. In fact, generally speaking, the higher up in the corporate ladder a person is, the more valuable they will be if they have a well-defined EQ. Beyond this general statement, those in human resources or public relations are likely to benefit the most from emotional intelligence at every stage of their careers. As such, proactively vetting these types of individuals for their current level of emotional intelligence can help maximize the contribution of new hires.

*EQ and the global economy:* Generally speaking, the global economy can be characterized by its high levels of communication, negotiation, and collaboration, which is why it is unsurprising to see that emotional intelligence has grown in importance as a result. Regardless of how the economy continues to grow in the future, conventional intelligence is going to continue to play a role. However, as it stands, even the roles most completely dedicated to technical proficiency require an increasing amount of contact with a wide variety of stakeholders which means EQ is crucial to dealing with the uncertain situations they sometimes find themselves in. That is to say, both rational intelligence and emotional intelligence are here to stay, and well-rounded leaders' exhibit and develop both of them.

*EQ and successful team building:* When it comes to building a successful team, emotional intelligence underlies the many effective processes that a reliable team can generate and while these results can be copied, their success cannot. This can be explained more easily by considering a competent art student. If this student were told to paint a copy of one of the great masters, the average person would not be able to tell the difference. They will never become the next van Gogh without understanding the theory behind the work and the soul that goes into it as well.

While creating a successful team requires more than just mimicking the process that has worked for others, by focusing on finding those with existing emotional intelligence you can create a scenario where the conditions are right for the team to develop successfully as a result. The conditions that are required in this scenario include a sense of group efficacy, group identity and trust amongst all its members.

What follows is a list of useful things you can do to foster these conditions in your own team:

1.  Designate a clear leader. Having a leader for the group who has a high EQ is crucial to helping the group reach its full potential. This will also prevent the group from wasting time and fracturing unity by having to decide on a leader for themselves. If you want this leader to be you, then additional to having a handle on your emotions and the emotions of others, you are also going to want to brush up on your conflict resolution skills so that you can end arguments without costing yourself the respect of the team as a whole.

Furthermore, you are going to want to get into the habit of always responding in a respectful, polite manner, regardless of the situation you find yourself in. A big part of this is listening more than you speak, which is a habit that few leaders cultivate as much as they should. A good leader asks for feedback and then takes what is given to heart when making future decisions. It is also important that you avoid making excuses and instead own up to your mistakes. Finally, you should make it a point to ensure that you become known as a leader that is willing to pitch in and lend a hand when it is needed.

2. Look for individual strengths and weaknesses within your team. As an emotionally intelligent leader, it is your job to ensure that you always think of your team as more than just cogs in the company machine and as more complex than their job title and function. While it can be difficult to retain focus while in the middle of a strict deadline, your employees are still unique individuals with skills to share and stories to tell. Much of the knowledge that they have

available to share isn't going to be readily available at first glance which means that it is up to you to get to know your team and thus bring out their full potential in the process.

When it comes to getting to know your team, it is important that you try and do so outside of the bounds of the project you are currently working on so that you can see the full breadth of what they have to offer. This means you will also want to look beyond the first impressions you might have of individual team members and use your EQ to find out who they really are. Generally speaking, you are going to want to make it clear that you approve of innovation and that it is rewarded with recognition. Additionally, it is important to make it clear that mistakes are fine, as long as something useful is taken away as a result.

**3.** As the leader, it is your job to ensure your team is passionate about whatever it is they are doing at the current moment. First things first, this typically goes much easier if you make a point of hiring people or building your team with people who are like-minded when it comes to corporate culture, and also passionate about the work they are doing at the same time.

Nevertheless, this doesn't mean that even the most passionate teams don't lose focus from time to time. To ensure you nip any sagging energy in the bud, you are going to want to make a point of recognizing the hard work your team has done, and not just superficially either, the team needs to feel like it is appreciated if you hope it to be passionate about its work. You may also want to use your improved EQ to develop alternate work environments that may engage the team more as a result. Finally, it is important that you do what you can to ensure that everyone understands the importance of the task in front of you and that they are unified in their desire to complete it.

4. As the leader, it is your job to create a team culture. When it comes to successfully managing the EQ of an entire group, you will likely find that it is often the smallest acts that make the biggest difference. This doesn't mean creating a scenario where employees don't feel comfortable going home at a reasonable hour or even creating one where every idea that comes up requires a deep dive into its meaning for the team as a whole. Nor is it about creating a space that is in complete unity and no one has any issues with anyone else, primarily because this scenario doesn't exist.

Rather, it is about creating a space where harmony is sought but not forced, tensions are released healthily and, above all else, everyone is treated with respect. While you will need to create rules from time to time, it is important to not do so without first ensuring that they connect to the core values of the team. You will find that when the guidelines you create support the beliefs of the team, as well as the goals of the company, everyone will feel more comfortable working to uphold the rules at all times.

5. As the leader, it is your job to find ways to manage the stress that comes along with the job. Too much stress can lead to even the most competent employees being burned out and can even lead to health problems if left unchecked. As such, it is important to be aware of the dangers of stress and do your best to deal with them before they arrive. To help keep your team's level of stress in check, consider trying the following.

## Chapter 9: Emotional Intelligence in the Workplace

First things first, it is always important to have a detailed schedule and stress the importance of sticking to it throughout the process. While giving a little extra time when it is needed is fine, seriously extending the deadline of a project can affect the team's ability to manage their time effectively in the long run. When creating a schedule, it is also extremely important to promote plenty of times for breaks so that your team can remain fresh and continue to work at maximum efficiency more of the time.

Generally speaking, you are going to want to avoid multitasking as for a majority of jobs it actually results in less, lower quality work being done than if each task was focused on individually. As such, instead of trying to get your team to work on more tasks at once, show your empathy and encourage them to work on one project at a time instead.

Additionally, it is important to keep in mind that not everyone is going to get along on your team, regardless of your best efforts. Luckily, you will find that taking the time to actively confront these issues and address them in an empathetic way is not only a great way to get to the heart of the matter once and for all, but it is also shown to reduce the stress to the team as a whole. Along similar lines, it is important to put your EQ to work to understand what really motivates your team, and then play to those strengths to help them overcome any challenges they may be currently experiencing.

**6.** As the leader, it is your job to ensure that every member of the team feels as though they have a voice and that their voice is heard. As the leader, this means it is your job to utilize your EQ to help them develop stronger communications skills, by allowing them to work on their active listening, gaining a better understanding of body language, and giving them a channel to vent their frustrations or concerns. This does not mean that you should give whatever negative emotions they are experiencing free reign, however, as they can drag the whole team down if allowed to remain unchecked. Instead, you should use the negativity as a chance to address the problem in the open, as a team, to come up with the best solution available.

**Choose your leadership style**

*Coercive leader:* A coercive leader is a very aggressive leader than needs to ensure that their EQ is at its peak if they want to ensure their team doesn't mutiny. They tend to get things done by dictating directives and ordering individual team members around directly, implicitly expecting compliance at every turn. This style is often effective among teams who work under dangerous or extremely time sensitive conditions when group discussions are not feasible. Those who pull of this leadership style successfully tend to have a reputation for success that justifies their harsh exterior. Teams that follow these leaders are often extremely close and group time away from work is a must to foster this type of group mentality.

*Authoritative leader:* An authoritative leader reaches their position because they have a vision for the future of the team that they can convince everyone else to get behind. This style of leadership can be effective if the team is currently having a hard time coming up with the best possible way forward. An authoritative leader needs to utilize their EQ in order to get everyone on board and focused in the right direction once more. They will also need to ensure that they get everyone to understand the importance of the big picture otherwise things can start to break down when they are not directly involved in overseeing them.

*Affiliative leader:* This type of leader is the best at creating a team that works with little external input. They make a habit of putting the members of the team first, no matter what and are often quick with positive feedback and praise as well. If a team previously had an extremely low opinion of one another and worked together poorly, this leadership style is a good way to improve bonding among the team while also improving overall performance. This style should not be used in the long-term as it easily let negative performance aspects go unreported in an effort to retain unity amongst the group.

*Democratic leader:* A democratic leader puts all the major decisions about the future of the team to the team itself. As such, it is important that the leader's EQ is where it needs to be in order to ensure that they can convince the individual team members that what the leader wants is actually best for the group, especially as they won't be able to do so directly.

Assuming the leader can handle the pressure, this type of environment allows employees to feel as though they are making a positive contribution to the team, heightening morale as a result. It can easily lead to unproductivity if not held in check by a strong leader, however, so it is important to approach it cautiously as it is a difficult leadership style to back away from while still saving face.

# Chapter 10:
# EQ Mistakes to Avoid

If despite your best your best efforts, you just can't seem to get your EQ to the place where you would like it to be, there may be some easily made mistakes that are slipping under your radar.

*Hiding behind labels:* While it can be easy to hide behind labels such as impatient, headstrong, grumpy and more. In reality, however, these labels are like calling a child who is obese big boned, it is sweeping a problem under the rug by slapping a politically correct label on it. These misleading labels are especially dangerous during the self-assessment phase of improving your EQ. Leaving certain major negative habits in place simply because "that's who you are" is a lazy and deceitful way of making things appear better than they really are and should be avoided whenever possible. If you have your doubts about a specific character trait, simply apply it to someone else and see if you still defend it so kindly.

*Socializing with the wrong crowd:* When it comes to your default mindset, those you spend time with on a regular basis influence how you think and what you value just as much as anything else including practice and exercise. What this means is, if you find yourself not taking to EQ improvement as quickly as you might have hoped you may need to consider who your primary relationships are with and how these other people view the world.

*Regretting things you cannot change:* If you find yourself regularly replaying back unsuccessful interactions in your mind solely so you can once again feel bad about the way you spoke or acted, then it is likely that your negative emotions are running around unchecked. Replaying these negative scenarios time and again will only give your mind extra outs when it comes to finding excuses to not try and improve your EQ the next time such a situation arises. This is a great opportunity to practice controlling your emotions more effectively, don't let it go to waste by allowing them to control you instead.

If you find it difficult to break yourself out of this type of pattern, rather than focusing on the situation in exactly the way it occurred, try looking back at the experience with a more clinical eye. Odds are you will find a weakness that you were previously overlooking or a path to success that you can utilize the next time you find yourself in a similar situation. Remember, it is important to remain on the lookout in these situations for longstanding beliefs that may need to be reconsidered. Only by monitoring yourself using a positive outlook will you be able to make the most of all the hard work you have already put in up to this point.

*Thinking about conversations in terms of winners and losers:* When you first start managing the relationships you have with others successfully, it can be easy to walk away considering yourself the winner of that particular social interaction. While there is nothing wrong with being pleased with yourself, thinking about conversations regarding winners and losers is a poor choice in the long run as it can ultimately lead to you taking each and every disagreement to the extreme in hopes of coming out on top in the long run. Regardless of what you may think at the moment, this is little more than a sign that your emotions are not actually being controlled properly as correctly utilizing relationship management means looking for the best outcome and working towards it no matter who contributed what to reach the current plateau. It is important to choose your battles and not live and die every time a difference of opinion occurs.

*Don't try and be perfect:* While improving your EQ will naturally make you more effective when it comes to navigating several crucial parts of everyday life, striving to have a perfect EQ will ultimately lead to failure. When it comes to working to meet a new goal, nothing sabotages the process more quickly than an unreasonable expectation. No one can ever truly be perfect at anything, and striving for perfection when it comes to EQ will only guarantee that you will eventually get frustrated at your lack of progress and give up on improving your EQ entirely.

What's more, EQ perfection is more than anyone needs, as long as you make a concentrated effort to work on the four pillars of EQ, then you will likely see all the results you could hope to make use of. Don't attempt to shoot the moon, set goals that will point you towards success, not a failure.

*Always giving into the needs of others:* When you are first working to improve your relationship management abilities, always agreeing to what the other person is asking for might seem like the best way to reach a consensus. While this might technically be true, it is not really in the spirit of what you should be trying to achieve in these instances, and you should focus on achieving a consensus that legitimately works for everyone instead. Even better, it will also help the other person to learn to respect you as a leader as opposed to feeling as though they can walk all over you instead.

While there are traditionally some negative connotations associated with saying no, the truth of the matter is that it is an important part of proper relationship management as it allows you an opportunity to work on retraining your natural impulses in such a way that creates expectations against instant gratification. It also makes it far easier to manage stress and also improve the way you handle your emotions overall. Generally speaking, it is also going to be better for everyone involved because you won't be committing to things you cannot realistically deliver on. Show respect for yourself and your time, say "no" when it is the right answer.

*No liking yourself enough:* When it comes to building up your emotional intelligence, it is important to get to know yourself as thoroughly impossible. If you ever want to become an EQ expert, however, then you are going to want to do everything in your power to ensure you really like yourself as well. For many people, once they have made a list of all their strengths and weaknesses, they don't care for what they are left with. Then, rather than facing their problem head-on, they make excuses for it, rationalizing away their weaknesses instead. Unfortunately, this is a temporary solution to a permanent problem which means that honesty is actually the best policy, especially when it comes to being honest with yourself.

Keep in mind that you are never helpless when it comes to dealing with your own weaknesses as the only thing standing in the way of your success is you. After all, everything that you are now is simply the result of all of your previous actions, nothing more and nothing less. If you keep this fact in mind, you will likely find that it is easier to create a plan that allows you to improve upon problem areas which will eventually lead to a new, and improved, you. Don't forget, the opinion you have of yourself matters more than that of anyone else, if you let yourself wallow in self-pity or apathy you will never successfully improve your situation.

*Using too many screens:* Studies show that a poorly timed push notification or text message can completely alter the mood of the person who is receiving it while at the same time naturally making them less receptive to the feelings and thoughts of those around them. This can directly negatively affect your ability to be empathetic to those around you which means you will need to do what you can in order to limit the amount of feedback you are receiving about your home life while you are at work and vice versa. Doing so will keep you properly focused on the relationships that are the most important at the moment and will keep negative thoughts from bleeding over from one sphere into the other.

If separating the two spheres proves difficult, you may want to double down on the mindfulness meditation, especially during your commute as this is sure to make the transaction between spheres easier to manage. Doing so will allow you to enter your work in the morning ready to face the challenges ahead and let you return home at night with the cares of the workday left behind.

*Incorrectly placing blame:* When it comes to choosing the best way to proceed in a given situation, there is nothing more potentially derailing then placing the blame for the situation in question where it doesn't belong. This creates an almost unsolvable problem as the wrong root will make it practically impossible to generate the outcome you had hoped for. Unfortunately, assigning blame can be tricky as both blaming others for their emotions and assigning that blame to yourself be each the right choice in certain situations.

If you blame others for their emotions in regard to your actions, then you are passing the blame to avoid dealing with personal issues. If you find yourself thinking that the other person is simply easily offended, then you may be looking at the situation in the wrong way. If you blame others for the way you feel without good reason, you are giving away the control of the situation you have. Regardless, the problem can be solved by taking the time to actively listen to the other person and working to get to the root of the problem. Clear communication is the easiest way to ensure blame lands where it will do the greatest amount of long-term good.

# Conclusion

Now that you have finished *Emotional Intelligence: A Step by Step Guide to Improving Your EQ, Controlling Your Emotions and Understanding Your Relationships*, it is time to stop reading already and to get ready to get started improving your emotional intelligence. Now, when reading through the proceeding chapters you likely came across exercises that you immediately saw the benefit in and others that you felt as though only benefit areas of EQ that you feel as though you have a fairly good handle on. Nevertheless, it is important to work through the exercises in the chapters in order for the best results. This is because the entire process is a gestalt, which means that it is more than the sum of its parts and working through each step will leave your

Emotional Intelligence

EQ more finely honed than it will be if you pick and choose the exercise you complete.

Depending on what level of emotional intelligence you have to start, it is important to keep in mind that it is likely going to take a fair bit of work before you start seeing any benefit, either in the way you handle your emotions of those or others. Nevertheless, it is important to stick with it as the only way you can ever hope to improve is with plenty of practice. Don't forget, improving your emotional intelligence is a marathon, not a sprint, slow and steady wins the race. Rather than looking to improve all facets of your emotional intelligence at once, you may find that you have better success focusing on a specific area that you want to change at a time, rather than working on everything all at once. Then, once you are confident in your new found skill you can move on to the next, bolstering its efficacy with what you have already learned.

While being empathic person whose emotional intelligence will soon be higher than average comes with a number of advantages, it also comes with added responsibility as well. With your newly honed emotional intelligence skills you have the ability to affect those around you, both for good or for ill. It is your responsibility to only use your skills to improve the lives of those around you and never for crass personal gain. Your emotional intelligence gives you the ability to be a force for light and good in the world, don't squander it. Don't forget, improving your emotional intelligence is a marathon, not a sprint, slow and steady wins the race.

# About the Author

Jessica Greiner is an author and a mother of two daughters. With a degree in Psychology, Jessica is passionate about helping people develop their inner emotional, psychic and sensual life. She believes that by understanding our brain and our emotions, why we do what we do, we are better equipped to deal with the various challenges we encounter in life.

Jessica writes books that are easy to understand and shares strategies that can be easily applied to everyone's day to day life. She has always been fascinated with the way people interact with others and the rest of the world. This interest has led her to the life of learning several factors affecting human interactions. Moreover, she continually works on expanding her knowledge by attending seminars and networking with other professionals.

When not writing, Jessica enjoys spending time horseback riding with her daughters or relaxing at the lake with her husband.

www.ingramcontent.com/pod-product-compliance
Lightning Source LLC
Chambersburg PA
CBHW020357130626
46549CB00006B/2316